THE WAY OF THE MAN

PRIEST - PROVIDER - PROTECTOR

30 Day Devotional

WHAT'S UP!?

I'm pumped that you're diving into this 30-day devotional based on my book "The Way of the Man." As someone who's been on a wild journey of discovering biblical manhood, I know firsthand how crucial these principles are - but also how challenging they can be to actually live out.

That's why I wanted to create this devotional as a companion to the book. It's not just about filling your head with more information. This is about transformation - allowing God to work in your heart and equipping you to become the husband, father, leader and disciple-maker that you know you're called to be.

Each day, you're going to unpack one of the key themes from "The Way of the Man" - from prayer and worship, to financial stewardship, to cultivating courage and compassion. You'll have a daily Scripture, a thought-provoking quote, and some reflection questions to get you thinking and praying.

The goal isn't perfection, my brothers. Heck, I'm still a work in progress myself! But it's about embracing the roles and responsibilities that God has uniquely designed us for as men - priest, provider and protector. I know those can feel like a lot of pressure, but I'm here to tell you it's not about an impossible standard. It's about stepping up and fulfilling the purpose that God has placed on our lives.

So don't just read through this thing passively. Dive in, engage with it, and get ready for God to do a new work in your life. Whether you're just starting out on this journey or you're a seasoned believer, there's something here for every man who's hungry to grow.

Now, let's get into it! Day 1 is all about the call to be a priest in your home and community. As 1 Peter 2:9 says, we've been chosen by God to be a "royal priesthood" - that means leading our families in spiritual growth and worship.

Take some time to reflect on what that looks like for you. How can you better fulfill your priestly role through prayer, Bible study and modeling authentic faith? What steps do you need to take to become the primary spiritual leader in your home?

Again, this isn't about becoming perfect, it's about humbly recognizing the responsibility God has given us, and then seeking His strength to step up and fulfill it. After all, as the quote says, "the highest calling of a man is to be a priest in his home."

So get ready to dive in, fellas. Over the next 30 days, you're going to be challenged, encouraged, and equipped to become the man God has created you to be. This is your roadmap for discovering The Way of the Man. Let's do this!

Your brother in Christ,

Troy A. Evans

DAY 1

THE CALL TO PRIESTHOOD

"But you are a chosen people, a royal priesthood, a holy nation, God's special possession, that you may declare the praises of him who called you out of darkness into his wonderful light."

- 1 Peter 2:9

REFLECT

What does it mean to you to be called as a "royal priesthood" in your home and community?

_____

_____

_____

How can you better fulfill your priestly role through prayer, worship, and guiding your loved ones?

_____

_____

_____

What steps can you take to grow in your spiritual leadership within your family?

_____

_____

_____

QUOTE

The highest calling of a man is to be a priest in his home."

DAY 2

A LIFE OF PRAYER AND WORSHIP

"Do not be anxious about anything, but in every situation, by prayer and petition, with thanksgiving, present your requests to God."

- Philippians 4:6

REFLECT

How would you describe your current prayer life and relationship with God?

_____

_____

_____

What spiritual disciplines can you incorporate to deepen your time of prayer and worship?

_____

_____

_____

How can you model a life of vibrant faith for your family and community?

_____

_____

_____

QUOTE

"The most important thing a father can do for his children is to love their mother."
— ***Theodore Hesburgh***

DAY 3

THE PROVIDER'S MANDATE

"But those who won't care for their relatives, especially those in their own household, have denied the true faith. Such people are worse than unbelievers."

- 1 Timothy 5:8

REFLECT

In what ways are you currently fulfilling your role as the primary provider for your family?

_____

_____

_____

How can you be a better steward of the resources God has entrusted to you?

_____

_____

_____

What steps can you take to ensure you are meeting the physical, emotional, and spiritual needs of your loved ones?

_____

_____

_____

QUOTE

"The measure of a man is not how much wealth he acquires, but the legacy he leaves behind."

- *Billy Graham*

DAY 4

THE PROTECTOR'S DUTY

"For we do not wrestle against flesh and blood, but against the rulers, against the authorities, against the cosmic powers over this present darkness, against the spiritual forces of evil in the heavenly places."

- Ephesians 6:12

REFLECT

How would you describe your current level of vigilance in guarding your family's spiritual well-being?

_____

_____

_____

What practical steps can you take to protect your loved ones from harmful influences and equip them to stand firm in their faith?

_____

_____

_____

In what ways can you cultivate greater discernment to recognize and navigate spiritual threats?

_____

_____

_____

QUOTE

"The greatest legacy one can pass on to one's children and grandchildren is not money or other material things accumulated in one's life, but rather a legacy of character and faith."

- Billy Graham

DAY 5

A MAN OF VISION

"Where there is no prophetic vision the people cast off restraint, but blessed is he who keeps the law."

- Proverbs 29:18

REFLECT

What is the vision God has placed on your heart for your life and family?

_____

_____

_____

How can you effectively cast that vision to inspire and motivate those around you?

_____

_____

_____

What practical steps can you take to align your goals and dreams with God's purposes?

_____

_____

_____

QUOTE

"A man without a vision is a man without a future. A man without a future will always return to his past."

- Zig Ziglar

DAY 6

THE IMPORTANCE OF DISCIPLESHIP

"And Jesus came and said to them, 'All authority in heaven and on earth has been given to me. Go therefore and make disciples of all nations, baptizing them in the name of the Father and of the Son and of the Holy Spirit, teaching them to observe all that I have commanded you. And behold, I am with you always, to the end of the age.'"

- Matthew 28:18-20

REFLECT

Who are the men in your life that you can invest in and mentor spiritually?

_____

_____

_____

How can you intentionally create opportunities to disciple others and pass on your faith?

_____

_____

_____

What are some practical ways you can hold yourself accountable in your own discipleship journey?

_____

_____

_____

QUOTE

"The greatest use of life is to spend it for something that will outlast it." .
— **William James**

DAY 7
EMOTIONAL HEALTH AND VULNERABILITY

"For we do not have a high priest who is unable to sympathize with our weaknesses, but one who in every respect has been tempted as we are, yet without sin."

- Hebrews 4:15

REFLECT

How comfortable are you in expressing your emotions and vulnerabilities as a man?

_____
_____
_____

In what ways can you create safe spaces for open communication and emotional support within your family and community?

_____
_____
_____

What steps can you take to cultivate greater emotional intelligence and empathy?

_____
_____
_____

QUOTE

"Vulnerability is not weakness; it is our greatest measure of courage."
- Brené Brown

DAY 8

TEAMWORK IN MARRIAGE

"Therefore a man shall leave his father and his mother and hold fast to his wife, and they shall become one flesh."

- Genesis 2:24

REFLECT

How can you better recognize and honor your wife's unique gifts and perspectives?

_____

_____

_____

In what ways can you foster a spirit of partnership and collaboration in your marriage?

_____

_____

_____

What areas of your marriage may require greater humility and a willingness to receive your wife's counsel?

_____

_____

_____

QUOTE

"*A good marriage is the union of two good forgivers.*"
- Ruth Bell Graham

DAY 9

PASSING ON A GODLY LEGACY

"Train up a child in the way he should go; even when he is old he will not depart from it."

- Proverbs 22:6

REFLECT

What are the key biblical values and character traits you hope to instill in your children?

_____

_____

_____

How can you intentionally disciple your kids and model Christ-like behavior for them?

_____

_____

_____

What practical steps can you take to create an environment where your family can thrive spiritually?

_____

_____

_____

QUOTE

"The greatest legacy we can leave our children is not money or material things, but rather an example of character and faith."
- Billy Graham

DAY 10

OVERCOMING ADVERSITY

"I can do all things through him who strengthens me."

- Philippians 4:13

REFLECT

How have past trials and challenges shaped you and equipped you for the road ahead?

_____

_____

_____

What areas of your life currently require God's strength and perseverance?

_____

_____

_____

How can you draw upon His power to navigate the difficulties you and your family may be facing?

_____

_____

_____

QUOTE

"Difficulties are meant to rouse, not discourage. The human spirit is to grow strong by conflict."
- **William Ellery Channing**

DAY 11

THE IMPORTANCE OF MENTORSHIP

"Iron sharpens iron, and one man sharpens another."

- Proverbs 27:17

REFLECT

Who are the mature believers in your life that can pour into you and hold you accountable?

_____

_____

_____

In what ways can you be intentional about seeking out their wisdom and guidance?

_____

_____

_____

How can you in turn invest in and mentor the next generation of godly men?

_____

_____

_____

QUOTE

"The greatest leader is not necessarily the one who does the greatest things. He is the one that gets the people to do the greatest things."

- Ronald Reagan

DAY 12

STEWARDING YOUR FINANCES

"The plans of the diligent lead to profit as surely as haste leads to poverty."

- Proverbs 21:5

REFLECT

How would you evaluate your current financial management and stewardship of resources?

_____

_____

_____

What practical steps can you take to develop a budget, save diligently, and use your finances to bless your family and further God's kingdom?

_____

_____

_____

How can you in turn invest in and mentor the next generation of godly men?

_____

_____

_____

QUOTE

"Wealth is not his that has it, but his that enjoys it."
- **Benjamin Franklin**

DAY 13

CULTIVATING DISCIPLINE

"Whatever you do, work heartily, as for the Lord and not for men."

- Colossians 3:23

REFLECT

In what areas of your life do you need to develop greater self-control and intentionality?

_____

_____

_____

What practical habits or disciplines can you implement to strengthen those areas?

_____

_____

_____

How can you approach your work and responsibilities as an act of worship to the Lord?

_____

_____

_____

QUOTE

"Discipline is the bridge between goals and accomplishment."
- Jim Rohn

DAY 14

GUARDING YOUR HEART

"Keep your heart with all vigilance, for from it flow the springs of life."

- Proverbs 4:23

REFLECT

How would you describe the current condition of your heart and inner life?

_____
_____
_____

What practices can you implement to regularly examine your motives, thoughts, and desires?

_____
_____
_____

In what ways can you surrender your heart to the Lord for purification and renewal?

_____
_____
_____

QUOTE

"The heart is the main battlefield; it is where the war is won or lost."
- John Eldredge

DAY 15

EMBRACING SACRIFICE

"Greater love has no one than this, that someone lay down his life for his friends."

- John 15:13

REFLECT

What areas of your life may require personal sacrifice for the good of your family or community?

_____

_____

_____

How can you cultivate a spirit of selflessness and a willingness to put the needs of others before your own?

_____

_____

_____

In what ways can you model the self-giving love of Christ in your relationships and leadership?

_____

_____

_____

QUOTE

"The measure of a man is not how much he accumulates, but how much he sacrifices."
- Michael Hyatt

DAY 16

LIVING WITH INTEGRITY

"The righteous man walks in his integrity; blessed are his children after him."

- Proverbs 20:7

REFLECT

How would you describe the overall integrity and authenticity of your character and actions?

_____

_____

_____

What areas of your life may require greater honesty, transparency, and uprightness?

_____

_____

_____

In what ways can you ensure your life and leadership leave a lasting, positive impact on your family and community?

_____

_____

_____

QUOTE

"Integrity is choosing courage over comfort; choosing what is right over what is fun, fast, or easy; and choosing to practice our values rather than simply professing them."

- Brené Brown

DAY 17

DEVELOPING COURAGE

"Have I not commanded you? Be strong and courageous. Do not be frightened, and do not be dismayed, for the Lord your God is with you wherever you go."

- Joshua 1:9

REFLECT

What challenges or fears are you currently facing that require greater courage?

_____
_____
_____

How can you draw strength from the Lord's presence and promises as you lead your family and community?

_____
_____
_____

In what ways can you model unwavering courage for those around you?

_____
_____
_____

QUOTE

"Courage is not the absence of fear, but the triumph over it."
- Nelson Mandela

DAY 18

CULTIVATING COMPASSION

"Therefore be imitators of God, as beloved children. And walk in love, as Christ loved us and gave himself up for us, a fragrant offering and sacrifice to God."

- Ephesians 5:1-2

REFLECT

How can you grow in your ability to see others through the lens of God's grace and mercy?

_____

_____

_____

What practical steps can you take to embody the compassion and self-sacrificing love of Christ in your relationships?

_____

_____

_____

In what ways can you create a culture of empathy and care within your family and community?

_____

_____

_____

QUOTE

"The measure of a man is how he treats someone who can do him absolutely no good."
- Samuel Johnson

DAY 19

PRIORITIZING FAMILY

"Husbands, love your wives, as Christ loved the church and gave himself up for her."

- Ephesians 5:25

REFLECT

How can you intentionally invest more time, energy, and resources into nurturing your marriage and raising your children in the Lord?

_____

_____

_____

What adjustments may be necessary to ensure your family remains your highest earthly priority?

_____

_____

_____

In what specific ways can you model Christ-like love and servant leadership within your home?

_____

_____

_____

QUOTE

"The most important work you will ever do is within the walls of your own home."
- *Harold B. Lee*

DAY 20

SEEKING ACCOUNTABILITY

"*Therefore, confess your sins to one another and pray for one another, that you may be healed. The prayer of a righteous person has great power as it is working.*"

- James 5:16

REFLECT

Who are the trusted brothers in Christ that you can invite into your life for accountability and prayer?

_____

_____

_____

How can you cultivate an atmosphere of transparency and vulnerability within these relationships?

_____

_____

_____

What specific areas of your life may require greater accountability and support from other godly men?

_____

_____

_____

QUOTE

"Iron sharpens iron, and one man sharpens another."

- Proverbs 27:17

DAY 21

MODELING GODLY LEADERSHIP

"Be imitators of me, as I am of Christ."

- 1 Corinthians 11:1

REFLECT

How closely do your words, actions, and attitudes align with the example set by Christ?

_____

_____

_____

What areas of your leadership may require greater examination and refinement?

_____

_____

_____

In what ways can you intentionally model Christ-like character and principles for those you lead?

_____

_____

_____

QUOTE

"The true measure of a man is how he treats someone who can do him absolutely no good."
- Samuel Johnson

DAY 22

EMBRACING YOUR IDENTITY IN CHRIST

"But you are a chosen race, a royal priesthood, a holy nation, a people for his own possession, that you may proclaim the excellencies of him who called you out of darkness into his marvelous light."

- 1 Peter 2:9

REFLECT

How would you describe your identity and sense of worth apart from your performance or circumstances?

_____

_____

_____

What biblical truths about your identity in Christ do you need to more fully embrace and live out?

_____

_____

_____

How can a deeper understanding of your identity in Christ impact your roles and responsibilities as a man?

_____

_____

_____

QUOTE

"You are not who you think you are. You are not who others say you are. You are who God says you are."
- *Louie Giglio*

DAY 23

PURSUING LIFELONG LEARNING

"The heart of him who has understanding seeks knowledge, but the mouths of fools feed on folly."

- Proverbs 15:14

REFLECT

What are some areas where you can dedicate more time to studying God's Word and seeking wisdom from mature believers?

_____

_____

_____

What books, podcasts, or other resources can you incorporate to foster continual growth and learning?

_____

_____

_____

How can a posture of humility and a hunger for knowledge equip you to better fulfill your roles and responsibilities?

_____

_____

_____

QUOTE

"The more I read, the more I acquire, the more certain I am that I know nothing."
- *Voltaire*

DAY 24

DEVELOPING SPIRITUAL DISCERNMENT

"But solid food is for the mature, for those who have their powers of discernment trained by constant practice to distinguish good from evil."

- Hebrews 5:14

REFLECT

How would you evaluate your current level of spiritual discernment and ability to recognize and navigate threats?

_____

_____

_____

What spiritual disciplines or practices can you implement to sharpen your powers of discernment?

_____

_____

_____

In what areas of your life or family do you need to exercise greater wisdom and discernment?

_____

_____

_____

QUOTE

"The greatest trick the devil ever pulled was convincing the world he didn't exist."
- **Charles Baudelaire**

DAY 25

LEAVING A LASTING LEGACY

"One generation shall commend your works to another, and shall declare your mighty acts."

- Psalm 145:4

REFLECT

What kind of legacy do you want to leave for future generations of your family?

_____

_____

_____

How can you invest time, resources, and energy into raising up the next generation of godly men?

_____

_____

_____

What steps can you take today to ensure your life and leadership have a lasting, positive impact?

_____

_____

_____

QUOTE

"The most important thing a father can do for his children is to love their mother."

- *Theodore Hesburgh*

DAY 26

OVERCOMING GENERATIONAL CURSES

"The Lord is merciful and gracious, slow to anger and abounding in steadfast love."

- Psalm 103:8

REFLECT

Have you experienced any negative patterns or strongholds passed down through your family line?

_____
_____
_____

In what ways can you find freedom and redemption from those cycles through repentance, forgiveness, and the renewing of your mind?

_____
_____
_____

How can you break those generational curses and leave a new legacy of faith and blessing for your descendants?

_____
_____
_____

QUOTE

"Generational curses only have power if you allow them to."

- Christine Caine

DAY 27

FOSTERING COMMUNITY

And let us consider how to stir up one another to love and good works, not neglecting to meet together, as is the habit of some, but encouraging one another, and all the more as you see the Day drawing near."

- Hebrews 10:24-25

REFLECT

How can you prioritize meaningful relationships and fellowship with other believers in your life?

_____

_____

_____

What are practical ways you can encourage and spur on the men in your community?

_____

_____

_____

In what areas might you need to be more intentional about participating in a supportive, Christ-centered community?

_____

_____

_____

QUOTE

"We are not meant to do life alone."

- Crystal Paine

DAY 28

STEWARDING YOUR GIFTS

THEME: USING YOUR GOD-GIVEN TALENTS FOR HIS GLORY

As each has received a gift, use it to serve one another, as good stewards of God's varied grace."

- 1 Peter 4:10

REFLECT

What unique talents and abilities has God entrusted to you? How can you use them to serve others and further His kingdom?

_____

_____

_____

Are there any gifts or skills you've been neglecting or underutilizing? What steps can you take to activate them for God's purposes?

_____

_____

_____

How can you cultivate an attitude of humility and gratitude as you steward the gifts God has given you?

_____

_____

_____

QUOTE

"God has given you gifts to use for His glory, not your own."
- *Rick Warren*

DAY 29

FINDING STRENGTH IN WEAKNESS

THEME: EMBRACING VULNERABILITY AS MEN OF GOD

"But he said to me, 'My grace is sufficient for you, for my power is made perfect in weakness.' Therefore I will boast all the more gladly of my weaknesses, so that the power of Christ may rest upon me."

- 2 Corinthians 12:9

REFLECT

In what areas of your life have you struggled to be vulnerable and authentic? How can you take steps to open up and share your struggles with trusted brothers?

_____

_____

_____

How can embracing your weaknesses and dependence on God's strength empower you to live more courageously as a man of God?

_____

_____

_____

Who are the men in your life that model healthy vulnerability? How can you learn from their example?

_____

_____

_____

QUOTE

"True strength is found in vulnerability."
- Anonymous

DAY 30

FINISHING STRONG

THEME: PERSEVERING IN FAITH TO THE END

"I have fought the good fight, I have finished the race, I have kept the faith."

- 2 Timothy 4:7

REFLECT

What are some areas in your life where you may be tempted to give up or lose heart? How can you draw strength from God's promises to persevere?

_____

_____

_____

Who are the men in your life that have modeled faithful endurance? How can you learn from their example?

_____

_____

_____

What spiritual disciplines or habits can you cultivate to help you stay the course and finish strong in your walk with Christ?

_____

_____

_____

QUOTE

"The race is not given to the swift or the strong, but to the one who endures to the end."
- *Unknown*

Made in the USA
Columbia, SC
05 September 2024